Voice from Afar

POEMS OF PEACE

BY **Tony Johnston**

PAINTINGS BY **Susan Guevara**

HOLIDAY HOUSE / *New York*

For my grandson
Noah Anjoh Wehrle:
I dream you a safe shore.
—T. J.

For Patrick O'Dell
and with much appreciation and gratefulness
to Alicia Allen, Julie Claire, Magio, Randy LaGro,
Victoria Rabinowe, Judythe Sieck,
and Nanette Stevenson.
—S. G.

Text copyright © 2008 by Susan T. and Roger D. Johnston Family Trust
Paintings copyright © 2008 by Susan Guevara
All Rights Reserved
Printed and Bound in Malaysia
The text typeface is Breughel Bold.
The art was created with acrylic and oil paint
with collage on textured canvas.
www.holidayhouse.com
First Edition
1 3 5 7 9 10 8 6 4 2

Library of Congress Cataloging-in-Publication Data
Johnston, Tony
Voice from afar: poems of peace / by Tony Johnston;
illustrated by Susan Guevara. – 1st ed.
p. cm.
ISBN 978-0-8234-2012-4 (hardcover)
1. Peace—Juvenile poetry. 2. Children's poetry, American.
I. Guevara, Susan, ill. II. Title.
PS3560.O393V65 2008
811'.54—dc22
2007031434

Contents

Voice from Afar

Child on the other side of the world,

child in some otherwhere,

standing in your little torn shirt,

I am calling.

Can you hear my voice?

There is an ocean between us.

And the sands of a desert.

Lean your ear as far as you can,

like a bird

that loves the wind.

Now can you hear?

Broken child in a broken land,

I dream you a safe shore.

For a Child

Whenever I rinse the plums
with cool water from the tap
above our little sink,
I look at each shining skin,
swollen with summer,
with rich dark honey.
I remember your sweetness.

Friend

The moon loves us, I think.
All these ages it has been faithful,
bestowing its luminous peace
upon us.

Chain-Smokers

A boy snatched the helmet
from a soldier who lay
crumpled in the street, a man
who only seconds before had lit
a cigarette and begun smoking
calmly.
The boy set the helmet on his own head
and smoked the cigarette
(ashes still glowing against
the day).
He puffed into the wide blue
sky, cocky as a bird. Then
a shot cracked; the sky
broke.

On the Road

Cap cocked jauntily,
a boy spoke to me. All I
remember: *Salaam*.

Afterlife

A small sign sags

against the fence of a house.

It is blasted to puzzle pieces.

The paint is strafed; you can hardly

make out the letters.

When you fit the shards

together, someone returns

from beyond the sorrow:

Welcome to my garden.

Any Direction Is Good

For Nazli Choucri Field

Nazli came to us from Cairo.
The day she arrived at our house,
she asked, "Which way is east?"
My little brother, ever the joker,
happily faced her prayer rug due north.

Six years she studied for her doctorate.
Six years she sank to her knees on the plush rug
and prayed faithfully to Allah, toward Oregon,
Alaska and the great Arctic Circle.

When Nazli discovered my brother's treachery,
she called him Little Stinker. Then she laughed.
No worries, Jimmy. North is good.
Wherever they are headed
all prayers reach God.

Overheard in a War Zone

Give us this day our daily bread
and, please, Lord, give us tomorrow.

Poverty

Where will the next bread come from?
And the milk?
Questions such as these are hulking,
big as the pyramids, in our yard.

Mother and Father only say: *There is hope*

as long as there is sky.

Inside our small house,
prayer beads, slick as lentils,
click against each other;
you cannot eat prayer beads.

Vagabond

I think of him sometimes,
the old dog—lost, dazed—
nosing along barren streets
for tidbits never found.
Once he lived in splendor,
nibbling delicacies from
a loving hand.

His ribs are the slats of a small ark,
visible to the stars
as he wanders
the famished
dark.

Sister to Brother

Tell me a story, a happy one.

Okay.
There was our squat little house
of good brown clay, standing
smack in the middle of a war.
Chunks had been torn
from its edges. By bullets.
And our little house missed
its edges quite a bit. So
it made a face
at the shooter.
Once a tank lumbered
down the street and pointed
its clumsy metal mouth
at our little house
and shouted, "Take *this*!"
and spouted fire.

So our little house just lifted
itself up, full of our mother and father,
grandmother and grandfather, and uncle
and me and you (in the bathtub,
scrubbing).
Like bread in the oven, it rose,
up, up, floating over the war.
And we all peered from the door,
clapping and crying and laughing and safe
in thin air.

Glory

Forgive my audacity, dear lentil.
But I know of a family—a few humble people—
who are hungry.
Do you think you might gather
several thousands of your closest relations
together, then spring into the soup pot
upon the fire of these poor people
like a moth flings itself into the flame
of a candle
and let them boil you and stir you
and eat you?
Should you agree, sweet lentil,
this would be a most glorious
gesture of goodwill.

Gone

Even though the house has been
                        shelled,
the stunned old woman keeps staring
at the rubble,
as though it might suddenly reassemble
                        itself.

When a Bus Exploded

Suddenly they are lost. So many.

They were soldiers maybe.

Or a shopkeeper in the midst of dusting.

Or rowdy children on their way to school.

Or solemn children, a boy and a girl,

tenderly clinging to their first love words.

Or a speckled dog dozing his days away in the sun.

Or a grandmother who only moments before

was sweeping the persistent leaves

that kept reeling down from the ancient plum

on their dry brown journeys into her yard.

Or a mother, pushing her laughing baby

on a swing the father made,

swinging it out into its whole wide life.

They are lost. So many.

Let none of them go unsung.

Plastic Shoes

The girl is dead.
Her life has flown off
like a sad little bird.
The body remains,
crumpled in the street.

One plastic shoe still covers
a foot; the other, a wink of blue,
is lodged in a pile of dirt.

How easily it slips
back onto her foot.

Magician

A father whose child

is dead

       leaps

atop the rumbling tank

frantically pulling

         doves

from a ragged

sleeve

of his striped

      bathrobe.

Gift

It is raining again.

Slopping the streets.

It is raining.

But people roam the roadways

as if there were sun

splashing every corner,

every inch of ground.

As if from every raindrop

flowers were sprigging up

from the parched and precious

pavements

of their town.

Belfast

*For Mary Bunting
and for her sons:
Ed, John, Fred*

She was laughing at some small memory

when she heard the crack of a shot.

A soldier fell wounded in the path.

For a long time he lay there.

But no one came near; no one dared help him—

for the snipers, bristling in the dark.

With the calm of the sea on a windless day,

my grandmother opened the door

of her house and strode toward the stranger.

Arms laden, she came, a little boat upon the water.

She placed a pillow beneath his head;

over him, the red shawl she had woven.

In delirium, he whispered, *Mother?*

Among the Sequoias

I am standing in the silence
of a grove of trees. Sequoias. Seedlings
millenniums ago. Now holy with years.

People are dying in far places
somewhere across the world,
the headlines blare.
Here am I muttering beneath the gaze of sequoias
my guilty prayer: *Keep my land beautiful.*
Keep my land safe. And my family.

Somewhere across the world
other people have spoken these words.
My family. My land, old and holy.
Keep. Oh, keep.

Somewhere people are dying,
or dead. I am muttering, but the words
somehow change themselves: *Keep all lands beautiful.*
Keep all lands safe. And all families.

My words lift from the trees
like birds.

Survival

Somewhere in Africa grows a rosebush
as tough as my little old grandmother.
We gave it to her, our family, when she
completed half a century.
We held a fine ceremony then and sang
and drank bush tea and ate gorgeous foods,
chapati, mandazi, kolas,
while each person gouged out dirt
to make a home for the rose.
My grandmother gingerly patted it.
Then she made a speech: *Little rosebush,*
now we plant you in the good earth. Grow.

Time passed.
Zealous clippers maimed the rose.
Dogs watered it. Storms mauled it.
Drought shriveled it.
War rolled over it. And peace.
But it always listened to my grandmother.
Always it came clawing back.

Rosebush, I will be like you:
Whatever comes, I will bloom.

Game of Peace

A ball rolls slowly up to a soldier
on patrol in a town.
A ball from an alleyway.
The soldier peers into the dark slot,
then gives the ball a boot.
He waits; the ball rolls back.
Again. Again.
Then, timidly, boys appear.
Back and forth, they whack the ball.
Their feet come to life.
Their eyes spark. They laugh.
The soldier's face remembers
it has a smile.
Nobody knows the game—
except the ball.

Ephemeral Bird

Peace skims the earth,
dips down, gently pecks
its cheek.
Then, in a wing-flick,
it darts away.
Before we can fill our
cupped hands up
with sweet seeds,
before we can entice it
to stay.

If Only

We will all go to the olive grove,

the one that stands on the lip

of our town, to create a plan

for peace.

I will invite everyone—

even our enemies.

Everyone will come.

My mother will bring

bread, fragrant with wheat

and warm from her round oven.

My father will bring cheeses

squeezed from the milk

of his nanny goats.

I will bring little sweet cakes

that I have made myself.

You bring something too,

all of you.

Then we will feast, taste

one another's foods

and talk all afternoon

of this and that,

it doesn't matter what.

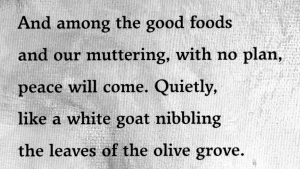

And among the good foods
and our muttering, with no plan,
peace will come. Quietly,
like a white goat nibbling
the leaves of the olive grove.

Let us follow the white goat
home.

Hope

The bird in the heart.

It is not ferocious. But—oh!—it is tough.

For a long time, through your life it sings.

It trills like a mad thing until

the walls around you are vibrating

with the glory of notes

and dreams become real

and you can feel them dancing

extravagantly on your fingertips,

swishing as supple as silk.

Then a school blows up in a bolt

of hate.

The world shrugs

and the little bird goes still.

Maybe it has only fainted;

perhaps it is just stunned.

Time passes. You cock your ear but hear nothing.

Then one day, when you are certain it is dead,

you hear a tiny eggshell sound. Like a dime

dropped into a blind man's cup.

You stop and listen with all your heart: *Peep!*

Salvation

A small red flower
—sprouting from the abandoned
boot of a soldier.

Let Us Weave

Let us weave something, you and I.
Together. Each seated at the border
of the loom.
We will use yarn,
the good wool of lambs.
No. We had better use something more
lasting.
Let us move the work quickly along,
tamping it down as we go.
You, with a wooden stick
made from the stock of a broken
gun; I, with the twisted shard
of a dead mine.
Let us weave something, you and I.
A new landscape.
A world
with peaks of kindness,
orchards branched with good,
rivers swollen with peace.